Dear Parent:

Your child's love of reading starts here!

Every child learns to read in a different way and at his or her own speed. Some go back and forth between reading levels and read favorite books again and again. Others read through each level in order. You can help your young reader improve and become more confident by encouraging his or her own interests and abilities. From books your child reads with you to the first books he or she reads alone, there are I Can Read Books for every stage of reading:

SHARED READING
Basic language, word repetition, and whimsical illustrations, ideal for sharing with your emergent reader

BEGINNING READING
Short sentences, familiar words, and simple concepts for children eager to read on their own

READING WITH HELP
Engaging stories, longer sentences, and language play for developing readers

READING ALONE
Complex plots, challenging vocabulary, and high-interest topics for the independent reader

I Can Read Books have introduced children to the joy of reading since 1957. Featuring award-winning authors and illustrators and a fabulous cast of beloved characters, I Can Read Books set the standard for beginning readers.

A lifetime of discovery begins with the magical words **"I Can Read!"**

Visit www.icanread.com for information
on enriching your child's reading experience.

For Aunt Ro
—L.D.

To all those who dream to fly
—C.E.

I Can Read® and I Can Read Book® are trademarks of HarperCollins Publishers.

I Want to Be a Pilot
Copyright © 2019 by HarperCollins Publishers
All rights reserved. Manufactured in China. No part of this book may be used or reproduced in any manner whatsoever without written permission except in the case of brief quotations embodied in critical articles and reviews. For information address HarperCollins Children's Books, a division of HarperCollins Publishers, 195 Broadway, New York, NY 10007.
www.icanread.com

Library of Congress Control Number: 2019937378
ISBN 978-0-06-243250-6 (trade bdg.) — ISBN 978-0-06-243249-0 (pbk.)

Typography by Jeanne Hogle
19 20 21 22 23   SCP   10 9 8 7 6 5 4 3 2 1
❖
First Edition

1 BEGINNING READING

I Can Read!

I Want to Be a
Pilot

by Laura Driscoll
pictures by Catalina Echeverri

HARPER
An Imprint of HarperCollinsPublishers

Bump!

Our plane touches down

on the runway.

"We are here!" I say to Aunt Ro.

I love airports.

I love airplanes.

I love everything about flying.

But today, the best part

is where we are going.

"We are going to the Air Fair,"
I tell the flight attendant.
It is a huge festival
all about air travel.

"I want to be a pilot!" I say.

"Just like Aunt Ro.

She flies an Air Force jet."

The flight attendant asks,

"Do you want to meet our pilot?"

Everyone else gets off the plane.

We go up to the front.

The pilot shows us the cockpit.

There are so many buttons
and switches.

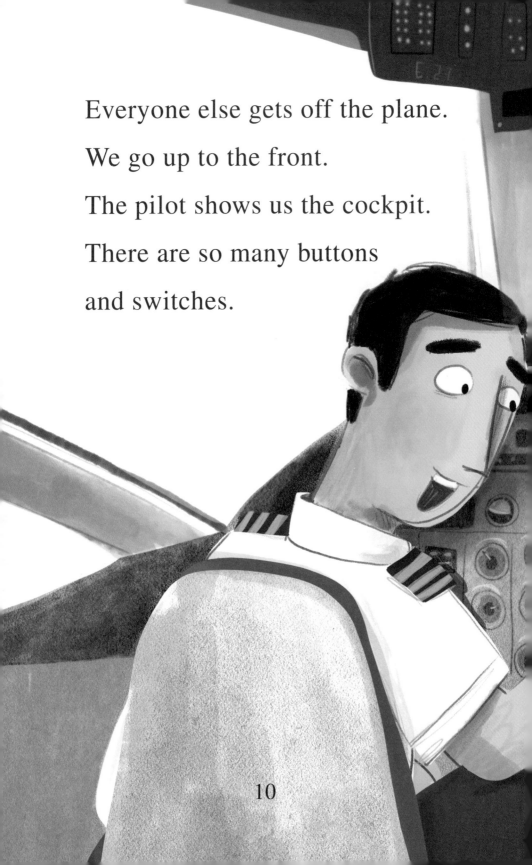

"You know what all of them do?"

I ask.

"That is my job," the pilot says.

"I do more than steer!"

11

"Before the flight, I check the weather," the pilot says.

"I plot the flight path.

I do safety checks
on the whole plane.

And I make sure I have some of these."
The pilot gives me a pin—
my own set of wings!

Soon we arrive at the Air Fair.

There are planes
as far as I can see!

14

We see a huge cargo plane.

We meet the cargo pilot.

"My plane transports things

instead of passengers,"

the pilot says.

"Most of our flights are at night,"
the pilot tells us.
"It is just me, my copilot,
and a plane full of stuff."

K-PZM

I sit inside a tiny seaplane.

The pilot is from an island.

"I fly people to the mainland,"

he says.

"I am like a cab driver

in the sky!"

Aunt Ro wants to see
the military planes
and meet other military pilots.

One pilot flies a transport plane.

"It can carry tanks, trucks—

even helicopters!" he says.

Then we meet a Navy jet pilot.

She can land her plane

on the deck of a ship!

And we meet a test pilot.

He test-drives new airplanes

to see how fast they can go!

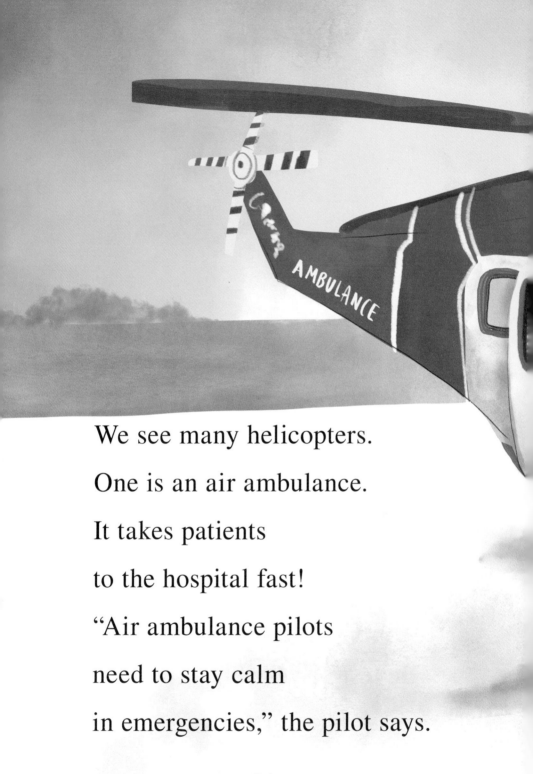

We see many helicopters.

One is an air ambulance.

It takes patients

to the hospital fast!

"Air ambulance pilots

need to stay calm

in emergencies," the pilot says.

We take a hot air balloon ride.

To steer, the pilot rides the wind.

He has to know

which way it is blowing.

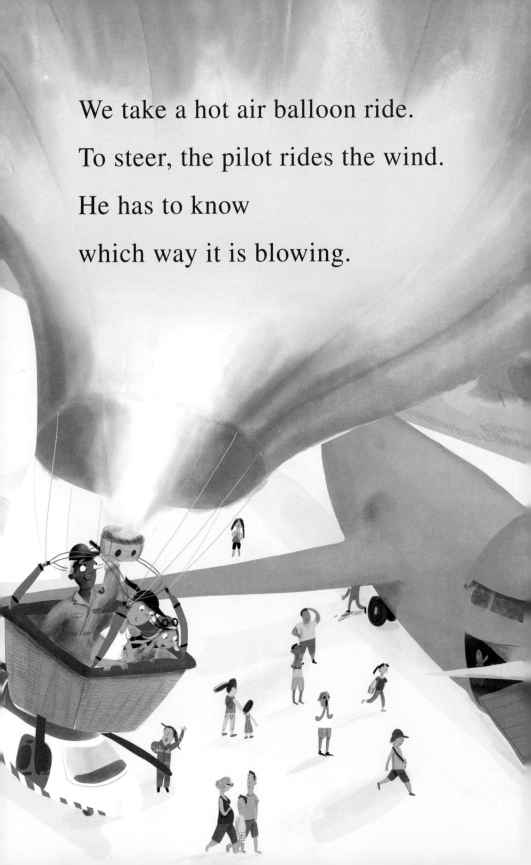

I look down over the fair.
I have met so many kinds
of pilots!

Aunt Ro takes me to meet

one more pilot.

"I'm a flight instructor," she says.

"I teach pilots how to fly."

Aunt Ro smiles at me.

"Are you ready for your lesson?"
Aunt Ro asks.

I can't believe it.

I am taking a flying lesson!

Will I like it?

I guess I will find out . . .

right now!

Meet the Pilots

Airline pilot
a pilot who flies passenger airplanes

Cargo pilot
a pilot who flies large airplanes loaded with packages and other shipments

Seaplane pilot
a pilot who flies planes that can land on water

Military pilot
a member of the armed forces who flies military jets, helicopters, or transport planes

Air ambulance pilot

a pilot who transports patients to the hospital

Hot air balloon pilot
a pilot who can fly a hot air balloon using knowledge of air currents

Flight instructor
a pilot who teaches others how to be a pilot